CONTENTS

The History of Games and Hobbies

Yesterday

A game or hobby is something fun that people enjoy in their free time.

Many years ago, children played simple games like cards and checkers. Then **factories** started making toys. Stores filled with dolls and **board games** like Monopoly.

Imagining the Future

At Play

in the PAST, PRESENT, and FUTURE

Linda Bozzo

OUR LADY OF PERPETUAL
HELP SCHOOL
7625 CORTLAND AVENUE
DALLAS, TX 75235

Bailey Books
an imprint of
Enslow Publishers, Inc.
40 Industrial Road
Box 398
Berkeley Heights, NJ 07922
USA
http://www.enslow.com

Bailey Books, an imprint of Enslow Publishers, Inc.

Library of Congress Cataloging-in-Publication Data

Bozzo, Linda.
   At play in the past, present, and future / Linda Bozzo.
      p. cm.
   Includes index.
   Summary: "Readers will learn about the history, present, and dream about the possible futures of different games and hobbies, such as baseball, dolls, roller skates, kites, board games, basketball, books, and playgrounds"—Provided by publisher.
   ISBN 978-0-7660-3436-5
   1. Games—Juvenile literature. 2. Hobbies—Juvenile literature. I. Title.
GV1200.B68 2011
790.1'922—dc22

                                    2010011595

Printed in the United States of America

062010 Lake Book Manufacturing, Inc., Melrose Park, IL

10 9 8 7 6 5 4 3 2 1

Illustration Credits: Brand X Pictures/Punchstock, pp. 3, 16 (bottom); Classic Stock/Alamy, p. 18 (top); Tom LaBaff, pp. 1, 7, 9, 11, 13, 15, 17, 19, 21; © Gregory Lang/iStockphoto.com, p. 5; Library of Congress, Prints and Photographs Division, pp. 2, 4, 6 (top), 12 (top), 14 (top), 16 (top), 20 (top), 22 (top); © Cat London/iStockphoto.com, pp. 14 (bottom), 22 (bottom); Photos.com, p. 20 (bottom); © Profimedia International s.r.o./Alamy, p. 8 (bottom); Shutterstock.com, pp. 6 (bottom), 8 (top), 10 (bottom), 12 (bottom), 18 (bottom); © Topham/The Image Works, p. 10 (top).

Cover Illustrations: front cover—Tom LaBaff; back cover—Shutterstock (bottom inset); © Topham/The Image Works (top inset).

Today

Times have changed. So has the way people enjoy games and hobbies. Families today have many exciting choices when it comes to how to play.

Tomorrow How do you think children will enjoy playing in the **future**?

1. Baseball

Yesterday

Baseball gloves were once small.

Today

Baseball gear has changed over time. Baseball gloves are bigger now.

Tomorrow

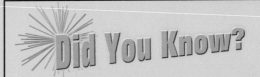

Did You Know?

The game of baseball was a favorite sport in the early 1900s.

How might baseball be different years from now? Will baseball gloves be even bigger? What if the bases light up to say that a player is safe? Computers might call balls and strikes. What will your favorite baseball team be?

2. Dolls

Yesterday

At one time, children played with simple dolls.

Today

Today, there are many different kinds of dolls to choose from.

Tomorrow

Someday dolls may act more like robots. They might be used for more than just play. What if a doll could walk your dog? Maybe it could check your homework. Would you like one that could play catch with you?

3. Roller Skates

Yesterday

Long ago, children strapped metal skates to their shoes.

Today

Today, children enjoy inline skates.

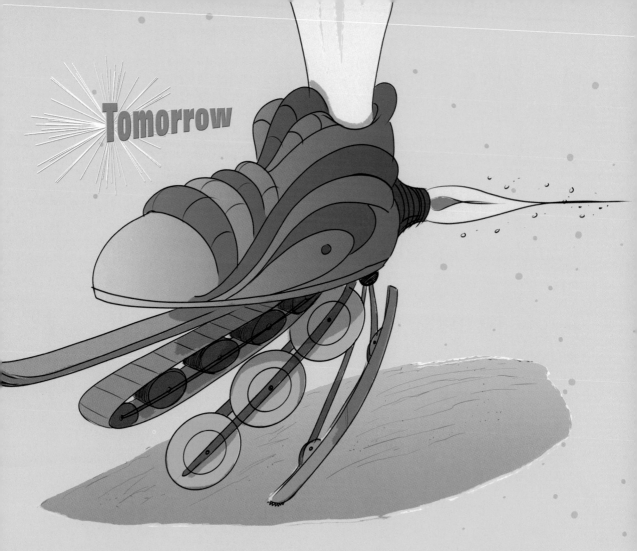

What if your skates could play music? What if
you could change the wheels? You could skate
on snow or ice. Change the wheels again. You
could skate on the beach. If your skates had
lights, you could even skate at night. Where
might be your favorite place to skate?

4. Kites

Yesterday

Children once used sticks, string, and paper to make simple kites.

Today

Today, most children enjoy flying kites bought from stores.

Flying high in the sky, kites might someday supply power. With a kite tied to your bike, you would not have to pedal. How far do you think you could travel on a bike powered by a kite? What else might kite power be used for?

5. Board Games

Yesterday

At one time, families enjoyed games played with cards, dice, and boards.

Today

Many people still enjoy playing these games. They also enjoy computer and **video games**.

What if one day playing a board game means
that you and your friends are zapped down to
a miniature size and become game pieces?

6. Women's Basketball

Yesterday

Once, women's basketball games were played using only half the basketball court.

Today

Today, women play basketball games using the whole basketball court.

Tomorrow

What if someday basketball courts had five baskets instead of two? What if they were higher? What if players had special goggles to help them see better and shoes with springs to help them jump higher? Do you think they would score more or fewer baskets?

7. Books

Yesterday

Reading books has been a hobby of children for many years. At one time, there were very few books for children.

Today

Today, there are many more books written for children.

Tomorrow

One day you might pick a book by just saying its name. Would you like a funny book? Maybe you would like a scary one. Whichever book you choose will appear in **3-D**. No need to hold it. It will float in the air. When you are done reading, no need to return it to the library. *POOF!* It will disappear into thin air. What kind of book would you choose?

8. Playgrounds

Yesterday

Many years ago, most outdoor fun di[d] not cost anything. Children often play[ed] on playgrounds that looked like this, wit[h] seesaws and slides.

Today

Today's playgrounds look very different, with climbing frames. New playgrounds are built over soft surfaces to make them safer.

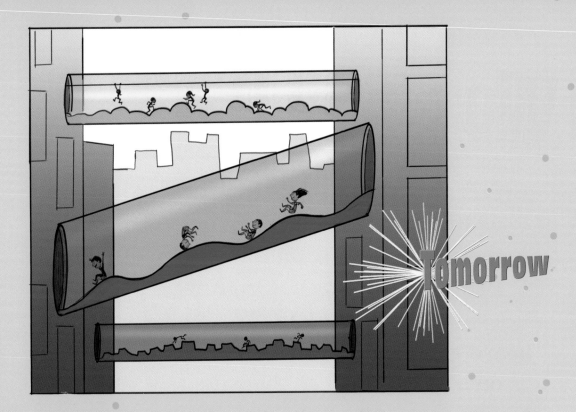

Have you ever wondered what playgrounds will be like years from now? What if they were more about exploring the world around us? With less open space, playgrounds might tunnel under busy streets. Tubes might take you over tall buildings or deep into the woods. What fun it would be if playgrounds were for adults as well as children.

The world we live in is always changing. No one really knows what will happen in the future. We can only imagine!

WORDS TO KNOW

3-D—Three-dimensional things have length, width, and depth. 3-D movies look as if things are coming off the screen into the room with you.

board game—Any game played on a board, such as checkers.

factories—Buildings where toys or other items are made.

future—The time after today.

video game—A game played on a television screen.

Learn More

Books

Easterling, Lisa. *Games*. Chicago: Heinemann Library, 2007.

Masset, Claire, and Felicity Brooks. *First Picture Playground Games*. Eveleth, Minn.: Usborne Books, 2007.

Yates, Vicki. *Having Fun*. Chicago, Ill.: Heinemann Library, 2008.

Web Sites

Astral Castle: A History of Board Games
<http://www.ccgs.com/games/index.htm>

Yahoo! Kids: Games
<http://kids.yahoo.com/games>

Yahoo! Kids: Sports
<http://kids.yahoo.com/sports>

INDEX